Enriching Life

Enriching Life

Hara Prasanna Das

PAPER MISSILE

NIYOGI BOOKS

Published by
NIYOGI BOOKS
Block D, Building No. 77,
Okhla Industrial Area, Phase-I,
New Delhi-110 020, INDIA
Tel: 91-11-26816301, 26818960
Email: niyogibooks@gmail.com
Website: www.niyogibooksindia.com

Design: Nabanita Das

ISBN: 978-93-89136-08-1
Publication: 2019

Printed at: Niyogi Offset Pvt. Ltd., New Delhi, India

Contents

Part – 1

Understanding Self

Understanding Our Talents

Understanding the Self is a difficult task. It is not as easy as it seems. How many of us have truly understood ourselves? Forget about the understanding of Self, let us ask, 'How many of us have ever tried to understand ourselves in every aspect? What is the meaning of Self?' We do hear tall talks on many occasions about self-motivation, self-development, self-awareness, self-realization, self-confidence, self-analysis and self-discipline. But we have very little understanding of the word 'Self' itself. How do we define Self? Self has always been a mystery. Search and research on Self by scholars all over the world have unfolded many of its facets. But the search is still on, as it is a never-ending process.

About Self

Let us come to Self. Before understanding Self, we have to answer many questions on it, such as: Who am I? What is my vision? What are my values? What is my goal? What is my role? What am I doing? What are my talents and strengths? What are my weaknesses? What do others expect from me? What do I expect from myself? Am I accountable to myself? Whom am I reporting to? Who is my guide?

The list is endless. The quest for understanding Self is never ending. The search will go on and on till one stops looking, or wrongly feels that he has understood himself properly. In the ancient times, saints left their homes and went to the forests to meditate and in search of Self. A few of them could understand the concept of Self, and hence, lead the society, which we live in now. But the search has not stopped till date. Social scientists, psychologists, philosophers and many scholars are involved in the search of and research on Self. Thousands of books and articles have been published on different aspects of Self.

All said and done, we have to make all efforts to understand ourselves. If we succeed in doing so, we can hope to develop ourselves. Self-awareness is the stepping stone to self-development. We must know where we stand. Self-awareness will lead to self-assessment, and eventually, to self-development. We should have a clear understanding of what we have and what we do. Let us go step by step in this direction of understanding Self. First of all, we must know our strengths, or say, our talents.

Talents/Strengths

Each one of us has many talents or strengths. Most of them are gifted at birth; we may call them genetic. A few, on the other hand, are acquired. Hence, we all are talented in some way or the other. But we rarely understand our inner talents. The reason is very simple. We have never made any serious or sincere effort to do so. We take ourselves for granted. We make ourselves believe that we know everything. We think that we are capable of handling anything that comes our way. We feel that we need not learn about Self, and hence, we pretend to be confident. But in reality, we are actually overconfident. That results in our failure, which in turn creates frustration.

We can look at our talents from five angles, based on its utilities: Talents fully utilized, talents partly utilized, talents unutilized, talents misutilized and talents not identified.

We may have talents, but those will not bring results until and unless used properly at the right time and at the right place. It again needs specific effort to use our talents as per the need and the situation. Theoretical knowledge is something we all have. But only those who know how to apply and where to apply the available knowledge, win. Similar is the case in utilizing our own talents. Successful people know how to utilize others' talents better than utilizing their own. This is called leadership skill. But leading Self is more important than leading others.

Self-analysis

Let us sit with a cool head and prepare the list of talents we have. This is called self-analysis. And then, put them into different groups as mentioned above. It is not at all an easy task. On many occasions, this self-analysis exercises have been undertaken by many in training sessions. Most of the times, these exercises were assigned as homework. Some have spent the entire night on this but weren't satisfied with the results. They felt that the understanding of Self is not at all a one-night task. Talking about it is always easy, but doing it in reality is tough. It is only when we go through the process, we realize the truth.

We can safely conclude that understanding Self is a lifetime task. One has to do it daily, like routine work, to get the best results. The picture of Self differs from event to event, from time to time. It is not clear cut. We cannot simply frame a common definition for this. Our thoughts and feelings determine our actions, which changes the concept of Self. That is why, sometimes, we behave in a way that we also do not approve of later. How does this happen? Hence, the common definition of Self will not at all work on all occasions. Regular interaction with Self with a positive attitude and creative thinking can only pave the way for understanding it in a better way.

Weaknesses

We all have weaknesses; let us call them our negative talents, which not only damage our life but also the entire society as a whole. But how many of us do admit this openly? When the time comes for us to own our mistakes, we try to escape and give many excuses. We do not hesitate to shift the blame on others for our mistakes. We always want to prove that we are outstanding, that we have no negative qualities. Can it be true in any case? No, not at all.

Hence, let us try to understand our negative talents—be aware of them well in advance before they damage our lives and others'. Let us admit that we all have negative talents. Having negative talents or weaknesses is not a crime; it is an intrinsic part of human nature. The crime occurs when we do not admit this, or we do not make any sincere effort to remove, control or manage them properly. Let us divide our weaknesses into five categories: weaknesses which can be removed completely, weaknesses which cannot be removed but controlled, weaknesses which can neither be removed nor controlled but suppressed, weaknesses which cannot be removed but rectified and, weaknesses which have not been identified till date.

Weaknesses are also talents, in a way. That is why we have mentioned them here as negative talents. These can be used as assets, at times. For example, you might be emotional as a person, but you can channel these emotions to be empathetic. Hence, we should never feel guilty of having negative talents or feel inferior to others or try to hide them. They are like bones in a fish. We have to remove the bones and savour the fish. Our mind has to be tuned accordingly.

Self-realization

Effective people have the habit of finding their own mistakes first, and then, correcting them before it gets too late. They are clever, as they do not wait for others to spot them. Before others spot our weaknesses, we must be wise enough to understand them ourselves and correct the same accordingly. This is what we call self-analysis based on self-realization. This is a continuous process, which is to be done every day, before we go to bed. Many of us have the habit of writing a diary or journal every day. This habit will help us find our own mistakes and shortcomings on a daily basis. Self-awareness about our negative talents will help us prevent many mishaps in our life. Negative talents will be there, but we must control or manage them. Hence, self-analysis is the appropriate path to understanding our own weaknesses, without any compromise. No excuses to ourselves should be accepted while analyzing our own lapses. It has to be done without any biases.

Managing Our Talents

No one is perfect, nor can be. Let us not be worried about that. But we can be excellent. All of us have both positive and negative talents; the ratio may differ from person to person. But they do exist at all times within us. Hence, the task is how to manage them effectively in our favour. No doubt, it is a challenge and we all have to accept it, face it and handle it with caution. Once we accept it as a challenge, we are mentally prepared to manage it as and when it comes our way. This is a continuous process, which is to be accepted as a part of our daily routine work—nothing more and nothing less. There are very few techniques to manage our talents to get better results. Some of these are self-analysis, self-realization and self-discipline. These are process and practice oriented. Hence, we have to practise these techniques regularly. Converting the negative talents to positive ones is the best way to find a solution to all our problems. This, again, is the fruit of regular practise. Let us start practising from today itself, before it gets delayed any further. We must remember that positive attitude is the key to all these practices.

The Art of Leaving and Living

Human life is perhaps the best creation of God, as we all believe. Each one of us loves his or her life. It is rare to find someone who does not. We all want to enjoy our life completely, in every aspect. All our efforts are to enrich the quality of our life. Given a chance, we rarely hesitate to live at the cost of others. Come what may, we wish to have the best of everything. We must make our life excellent at any cost, is what we think and want. Hence, we are eager to learn the Art of Living, as quickly as possible.

We are interested in the output or the end result. Our focus is on what we get at the end. We call it 'achievement'. In the present fast-paced life, everyone is interested in grabbing that end result as quickly as possible. And also, we do not compromise on quality. But the tragedy is we barely realize that the process is more important than the result. The excellence in the output entirely depends on the excellence of the process. All events are the results of different processes. Hence, the focus has to be on the process first, if at all we want to get the desired result. How many of us realize this and act accordingly? Life is a process. The journey from creation to cremation is what we call 'life'. Life is not the end result. It is a gift of God. We should take care of our life and make the best of it. The end result depends on how we use our life, better to say, how well we act on the process. Life is based on the concept of input vis-a-vis output. The harvest is linked to our investment in life. As we sow, we reap. The investment of our time and talent, mind and heart, body and soul in the right direction makes our life effective, qualitative, peaceful, happy, enjoyable, remarkable and successful.

Interestingly, most of us take risks by investing our money in share markets, though we are sure that sometimes we may lose heavily. But we still dare to take that risk with the desire of making more profit in that investment. We develop an interest in the investment of our money, which we consider an asset. But the real assets are our time and talent, which need proper investment in life. These are the gifts of God. They cannot be bought. Investment of time and talent is not an one-off event; it is a lifetime of work. Acceptance of this truth will make our work towards achieving a meaningful and effective life easier.

The art of living cannot be effective if we do not learn and practise the Art of Leaving. If we want to live happily, we must leave many things happily, too. It is a known fact that we have to make many sacrifices in order to get our desired goal. But we are not prepared to do so. If you get detached from one, only then can you be attached to another. Hence, we must leave all our negative traits such as anger, jealousy, ego, greed, possessiveness, selfishness, immoral activities, lies, indiscipline, corruption, argument, enmity, negative attitude, ill feeling for others, etc. Thereafter, we will be able to imbibe all the positive factors needed for a happy life.

We mostly use our mind as a waste basket, collecting all evil thoughts and ill feelings. These fill our mind and heart so much that there is no place for positive thoughts. The negative vibrations expel all positive ones from our mind. Our mind, thus, gets polluted and we become mentally affected. Hence, we must convert our mind into a flower basket and start collecting the best blossoms, from all sources. Hence, let us practise the art of leaving from today. We must think and realize deeply to prepare the action plan for this. What to leave, when to leave and how much to leave are the most important factors in the art of leaving. We must focus on these areas with all sincerity and dedication. It is not as easy as we think. It is a tough task and needs to be taken as the true challenge of our life. Realizing its need and importance, and accepting the truth in the art of leaving is the first step in learning the art of living.

The Four Pillars of Love

'Love you, love you and love you.' Saying this alone has no meaning. We have to prove it in action. But how many of us truly prove it with bold conviction and positive action? Perhaps, a very few only take the risk and face all challenges to show it in action, instead of just words. Come what may on the path of true love, we must march ahead, without giving it up halfway. We all know this but very few realize the truth and act accordingly. Love is the foundation of life. It acts like a bond that holds all of us in a relation, be it personal or professional. We will explore here the four pillars of love, which make our life more meaningful and joyful.

Love Self

We love our near and dear ones so much that we always focus on their betterment. We take all care to find their lapses and correct them. We strive to add value to their life. But at the same time, we forget to find our own lapses and correct them for the improvement of Self. Most of us have not understood

Self from all angles. We know very little about our Self, because we have not given adequate time for self-awareness and assessment. As observed in many cases, we have neglected ourselves and damaged our own life. With our casual approach, and sometimes with overconfidence, we waste our time, talent and energy with zero effect. We are the architect of our own life, but we ignore this aspect, and hence, do not achieve our goal as desired. Hence, we must love our own Self first and make the best use of our talent, time and resources.

Love Work

Work is worship, is the common adage. Work is the means to reach our goal in life. Work makes our life fruitful and meaningful. Work is our identity. Life starts with work and ends with it, so does a day in our life. Getting up in the morning is a work; going to bed at night is also a work. We work to live and live to work. We create our identity through work. We are either praised or rebuked for our work. But many a time, we consider work as a burden and avoid it. In order to make our life effective and joyful, we must love our work. If we love our work, we will enjoy the work and learn to do it better. We can enrich our life through work only. Hence, we must love our work and strive to excel in it.

Love Others

As stated by Swami Vivekananda, selfishness is immoral and selflessness is moral. As long as we are selfish in our action, we cannot love others and cannot receive love from others. We must love others and accept others as they are. We are all creations of God. We have the Divine power. No one is perfect. Each one of us has both positive and negative qualities. As we love ourselves, we must love others, too. Then, we will get mental peace and live happily. We will achieve this if we can forgive the mistakes of others. We must give up our ego, negative attitude and selfishness, so that we can love others.

Spread Love

One of the missions of our life should be to spread love. Happiness increases when you spread it and knowledge increases when you share it. Similarly, love is enriched when you share it. Love is the only binding force in all interpersonal relations. Love can wipe the tears of others and put a smile on their face. Love can cure diseases and heal injuries. Love can work as a magic and create the scope for living a pleasant life. We do not lose anything by sharing love but get many things in return that make our life more valuable. Hence, never forget to share and spread love.

A building may not have four walls, but it needs four pillars to keep the roof in place. Hence, the four pillars of love form the foundation of our life.

Leading Self Is the Best Leadership

'Leadership' is a very commonplace term. It needs no elaborate definition. Leaders practically do not need any introduction; rather, they are easily identifiable in all sectors of our society. Be it self-claimed or recognized by others, leaders are easily visible. Some people claim themselves to be leaders and some are genuine ones, accepted by the people as so.

Generally, leadership is considered as the act of leading a team/group, a family, an organization or even a state or a country. Leadership is the ability to lead others. It is a special quality, which is observed in a very select few. Some are of the opinion that leaders are born, not made.

Each one of us has leadership qualities. We can take the example of anyone in the society—starting from the illiterate to the literate, the rich to the poor, male or female, a child to an old man. One may not be leading a team, group or mass of people, but it is a fact that each person is leading himself or herself, in some way or the other. Generally, we ignore this fact of leading Self, which is the natural truth in our life. We are ourselves every day through each action to keep ourselves alive. This is the bright example of leadership. Hence, true leadership is leading Self in the right direction with a positive attitude to achieve our goal. Each one of us takes his or her own decision, just like a leader. We face challenges, take risks, solve problems, ask for help from others and think creatively to plan our life in a better way. Is it not leadership? We are all born leaders. These leadership qualities are to be enriched to empower ourselves.

The joke of the time is that the so-called leaders in our society are mostly not genuine; it has been proved many a time and on many occasions. This needs no further explanation. People with negative qualities are occupying positions of power in different areas, simply through networking. Interestingly, it is observed that they focus on their individual benefit and growth, instead of the interest of the masses. This clearly proves that the leadership is neither well defined nor understood properly by them. They are not the role models of genuine leadership.

Let us make it clear, again, that we are our own leaders. We must learn and practise to lead ourselves in the best possible ways. Under any circumstance, we will neither underestimate ourselves nor will we become the blind followers of the so-called 'leaders' in the society. We must empower ourselves to think creatively and feel positively. We should nurture our natural ability to decide our own course of action. We cannot change others, but we can change ourselves for the better. Leading Self is the best leadership. Hence, we must develop our leadership abilities to lead ourselves for a more meaningful and peaceful life.

Embracing a 'No' with a Smile

'Yes' and 'No' are the two sides of a coin. Be it personal or professional, when you take a decision on any issue, it has to be either Yes or No. But it becomes difficult for some to take a clear decision. They waver between Yes and No. They are indecisive, unable to take a decision, either this side or that. We always need to take a thoughtful and positive decision. It may be 'Yes' or 'No', depending on the situation. There is no escape from this.

Mostly, we feel comfortable with the Yes factor and just the reverse with No. By default, we are not mentally prepared to accept 'No' for an answer (when we want to hear a 'Yes'). Similarly, we hesitate to say 'No'. There are some people who simply cannot accept 'No' from others, on any occasion. Truly speaking, most of us are allergic to the word 'No'. This attitude creates problem.

Hence, we should learn how to accept No positively, with a smile. A few examples of embracing the No factor are described below.

Accept 'No' Positively

We may be expecting to get a Yes from others in a few cases, but if we get a No, we must accept it positively, too. Reality is what we get but not what we expect. Hence, when we get a No, we should neither react nor resist nor get affected. First of all, we must accept it positively, then think and analyze the practical side of it. With a cool head, we can take a right decision for the next course of action. We must remember that we can't demand a Yes from others, always. We cannot expect people to conform to our views and philosophies at all times, nor can we expect them to give in to our whims and fancies.

Learn to Say 'No' Creatively

We have emotions, but we should not do anything emotionally. Even if we feel like saying 'No', we refrain from doing so, owing to emotional reasons. But for how long can we hide the reality? If the situation demands a 'No' for an answer, we must say so. We have to be very down to earth and pragmatic in all situations. Saying 'No' may be a little difficult, but we must learn that art. It may be uncomfortable at that moment (as we do not like to hurt others' feelings), but it will make everything better in the long run. We must learn how to accept the reality, which may be a No instead of a Yes.

Never Focus Only on 'No'

Most of the people focus on the No factor and prepare a list of Nos in their life. They retain it in their mind, discuss, debate and share it with their friends and relatives. They get wrapped up in the list of Nos and invite all frustrations. They lose their confidence and courage to progress further. Hence, we must focus on all the Yes factors and get motivated to work with more courage and confidence. We must develop the habit of focusing on successes, and not failures. An optimistic attitude is always a great place and way to start.

Say 'No' to Self

With excitement and emotions, we often take wrong decisions, which we realize later on. But by that time, we damage ourselves. Naturally, we are unable to control ourselves on many occasions, which lead us to taking wrong decisions. Self-discipline and self-restriction are the best tools which will prevent us from moving in the wrong direction. So, we must learn how to say 'No' to ourselves, too. In case of all excitement, temptation and emotion, we must be able to convince and control ourselves. This is the ability to say 'No' to Self.

Convert a 'No' to a 'Yes'

No doubt, we all love to accept the Yes factor, but No is also a reality. Neither can we demand a Yes from others, nor can we prevent others from saying 'No' to us. Reacting to or resisting a 'No' will not solve the problem; rather, it will aggravate it. The better option is to think of converting 'No' to 'Yes'. When we keep our heart clean and head cool, we can find ways and means to convert No to Yes. Nothing is impossible. We have to think creatively and positively with confidence.

There is no end to situations where we will be confronted with No, instead of Yes. Hence, we must learn to accept a No and embrace it. If we learn and practise the actions mentioned above for dealing with the No factors in our life, we will definitely lead a peaceful and effective life, in spite of all hurdles. Let us embrace the No factor from today.

Life is Simple, But...

Simple living and high thinking was the motto of Mahatma Gandhi, which we quote with pride even today. Life is very simple, but we make it complicated. Perhaps, it is very difficult to be simple. We all know it, but we do not realize the significance of simplicity. Simple living is peaceful, meaningful and joyful. But why do we mostly prefer to be complicated? Is it that difficult or not desirable to be simple? Thousand and one questions arise on this when we start debating. Here, we will discuss three ways in which we can keep our life simple, rather than making it complicated.

Admitting Our Mistakes

No one is perfect. We all commit mistakes. Hence, admitting our own mistakes is not a failure or defeat; rather, this is a magnanimous act. We can learn a lot from our mistakes; they can enrich our knowledge, skill and attitude. We grow and learn when we admit and act on our shortcomings. But most of us prefer to hide our mistakes by trying to justify or explain them.

When someone finds our mistakes or lapses, we instantly react and try to justify our stand—as if acknowledging a mistake is a crime. If we have the courage to admit our mistake, we can learn from them and never repeat them in the future. In the process, we add value to our life. It is as simple as that. But we prefer not to admit it but to fight for that. Denial never helps.

Speaking the Truth

Truth is its own reward. It has enormous value. Truthful persons are held in high regard in society, at all times. But why do we prefer not to speak the truth, rather lie very easily? Some people even consider it as a courageous act. We say something on the face and act just the opposite. Then, we justify that action with many lies, properly coined to cover all truth. Hypocrisy is preferred over transparency. Presently, 'transparency' is the most honoured word in the world of management. Each one of us claims to love transparency but in action, it is not. Speaking the truth is a very simple act. We must have that positive attitude and courage to be truthful. But we prefer to hide the truth and create all confusion in life.

Keeping Our Calm

Presently, the entire world has started realizing the importance of staying calm and collected, even in the face of adversities. Meditation and yoga are gaining importance across the world. The struggle for existence has become tough and hectic, thus polluting our mind, besides all other forms of pollutions. Any event in our life never creates a problem, but our reaction to that event creates all troubles. Hence, we must have control over our attitude towards all issues and events in life. It is better to respond than to react, which will prevent most of the troubles. Keeping our heart clean and mind cool is the first step in leading a peaceful and joyful life. It is very easy to react but very difficult to respond rationally. It can happen if we realize the charm and worth of being calm and composed.

We must admit that we are the architect of our own destiny; either we make it or break it. Everything depends on what we think and feel, and how we act/react. We have to own the responsibility of being the master of our destiny. If we have the spirit to understand everything in a positive way, we can lead a very simple life, coupled with peace, joy and good health. Let us try to be simple and enjoy each moment of our life.

An Effort to Be a Professional

Excellence is what we expect to achieve in all our activities, thus making it the goal of our life. But most of the time, this does not happen. We feel discouraged and depressed, and blame others for our failure. We rarely make efforts to find the reason for failure, which is usually within ourselves. We never want to discover our own mistakes or admit to making them. We prefer to blame others, even our fate (God) at the end. Then, we take the shelter of astrology and other such means to ensure that we achieve excellence in all future projects. Subsequently, we realize this is not the right path to achieve excellence in life.

Most people have a casual approach towards their work, without any seriousness, and still expect success. A careless and superficial attitude towards work will never pave the way for excellence. We have to think and act like a professional. Professionalism is, indeed, a matter of how we do things, rather than what we do. It is an attitude that influences standards, ethics and processes. It defines what we stand for and what we stand against. The following are a few telltale traits of a professional.

Owns Responsibilities

A professional owns the responsibilities of work assigned to him/her; he/she never waits for anyone to give it to him/her. As such, responsibilities are not given but taken. Duties, which is the traditional way of doing things, are allotted. Duties can be documented but not the responsibilities. The sense of responsibility comes from within. A professional takes on responsibility, creates the opportunity for work and performs more than is expected of him. He loves to take additional responsibilities and finds ways to perform with excellence. A professional creates a climate of trust in Self as well as in others. So, others also put their trust in him/her.

Admits Mistakes

The best quality of a professional is that he/she admits his/her own mistakes; he/she takes pride in doing so. It takes maturity and courage to admit making mistakes, which most don't have. Instead, they protest, react and justify their wrong doings till the end. They waste their time, talent and energy in explaining the reasons for that action but never admit their mistakes. But a professional admits his/her mistakes and learns from them, so as not to repeat the same again in the future. This ensures better performance. The truth is that no one is perfect and we will commit mistakes. Admitting mistake will ensure better work.

Surrenders to Work/System

A professional loves to surrender himself to his work or the system. He never wishes the work or the system to surrender to him. Many people focus on Self but not on their work. They wish that the work must be undertaken as they desire. They try to change the system or the work as per their suitability, and not the other way around. They are not ready to change themselves to get the work done in a better way. They have their own mental blocks or rigidity of mind. They are obstinate. But a true professional focusses on the work and its quality. Hence, he/she changes his/her strategy, approach and plan of action to induce better performance. He works as per need of the system and the work assigned.

Love for Work and Focus on Goal

A professional enjoys doing his work. Work is not a burden for him. He has the focus on his goal, always. He is well composed and balanced. His concept about the work assigned is very clear. A professional never looks for reasons, or rather, excuses, for not doing the work. Instead, he finds all the reasons to get quality work done, in time. As he is focussed on his goal, he works towards achieving it. This is the secret of success. They fix their goals and plan their actions around it, and too in a professional way. They never compromise on the work process and quality standard. Hence, they achieve excellence.

Being a professional is an art and it takes hard work. Let us work towards trying to be one, irrespective of our field of work.

Part – 2

Managing Self

Do We Have Trust in Ourselves?

Do we have trust in ourselves? The question is very simple but the answer is not. Once, I asked this question to one of my very close friends. Surprisingly, he gave a very spontaneous answer—'Why not?' I explained to him that this is not the answer to my question, as this (Why not?) is again a question. I emphasized that the answer should be a 'Yes' or 'No'. My friend laughed and answered: 'Of course, yes.' I didn't agree to that answer. With all patience, I asked him, again, 'What is the need of adding "of course" to your answer "Yes"? If you are confident that you have trust in yourself, then the answer in the first instance should have been "Yes". Because you are not sure of that, your answer is of a different nature.'

Subsequently, I asked this question to around fifty people from different categories such as age, gender, education, unemployed, self-employed, well off, economically backward, etc. More than 80 per cent of them were confused. Instead, they asked me about the justification of such a question. The question was very simple for them, but it was too difficult to give the appropriate answer. The wide range of answers, or rather responses, from those people clearly indicate that they were not sure about their trust in themselves. Precisely, we can say that they were not confident about themselves.

We have never seriously thought on this issue. We are prompt in expressing our views on others—their actions, their character, their judgement. But when it comes to Self, we hesitate to express our views boldly and honestly. This difference in our behaviour is the result of our weak personality. While we are bold enough to expose others' weaknesses, we are weak in trying to hide our own. This clearly indicates that we do not have trust in ourselves. On many occasions, we are confused how to act. We are in a fix between yes and no, to do or not to do, to say or not to say, etc. The reason is that we are not prepared to take a risk. We are indecisive. We feel insecure about our own decisions. We go on asking our so-called well-wishers but do not feel comfortable taking the right decision boldly, at the right time. Does it not prove that we do not have trust in ourselves?

'Trust' is a very familiar and sensitive word. Trust defines the credibility of a person, or an organization. Intimacy in a relationship is measured by mutual trust. The word 'trust' adds value to all activities in our life. Hence, we use it on many occasions to prove our authenticity and also to glorify our worth. But the greatest tragedy is that the word 'trust' is misused on many occasions. Very often, we motivate others to have trust in us, in God and also in others. We even claim that we have trust in our own people. But in reality, neither we have trust in ourselves, nor in God, nor in others. Having trust in someone is now a relative term, directly or indirectly connected to ones' personal benefits.

Let us accept that we should have absolute trust in ourselves. Then, we will not be in any confusion on any issue. We must have the ability to think, feel and realize with confidence to take appropriate decisions. Whatever may be the output, we should comfortably and boldly take a decision, without any hesitation. We can take any risk. We can face the challenges with a smile. We can accept the reality of life, be it positive or negative. We can have a cool head tuned to embrace all uncertainties at each stage of our life. Positive attitude and creative thinking will be the foundation of our decision making. We can lead a balanced life in both personal and professional fields. Hence, there will be no stress, no tension and no disease. But in the present society, why is this not possible?

The reason is very simple; we do not have trust in ourselves. Why not think over it deeply and try to realize the validity of such a question? Hopefully, we can find the right answers.

Self-analysis Leads to Self-development

Self-development is a common goal in everybody's life. We cannot find a person who is not interested in self-development. Each one of us is interested in complete development, in both personal and professional life. Substantial growth in every aspect of our life is much desired. But, how do we achieve this growth or development?

Talking about development is simple, but it is difficult to find the correct ways and means to achieve it. Different people adopt different strategies, paths, processes and tools—as per their suitability—to achieve development. But most of the times, it does not click. The reason is very simple. There is no shortcut to development. Different schools of thoughts have suggested some common and basic paths for achieving development, especially for self-development; the most vital path being self-analysis. Self-analysis, coupled with a positive outlook and creative thinking, will definitely lead to self-development. Self-development can be broadly divided into these four categories:

Input

We all dream of excellence. If we do not get what we expect, we become depressed or have negative thoughts. But a very few of us analyze the inputs we have invested to get the desired results. The inputs may be time, talent, energy or any resource relating to that particular work. Hence, the first stage in self-analysis is to find out the details about our inputs. Life is based on simple input and output principle. This truth is known to all, but we run after the illusion. Hence, we must analyze and assess the quantum of our resources invested. We must document them properly in order to convince ourselves about the reality. We must remember that output depends on input. Hence, the amount of input can be revised accordingly for better productivity.

Output

All our input into any work lead to the output, which may be as per the expectation or otherwise. Hence, at the end of the day, we have to prepare the list of our output. Those are our achievements on that day. We may accept it or not, but that is the results of our efforts. The output may not be always as per our expectations, but they have their own worth. All achievements must be assessed in a positive way. Some achievements may seem meaningless at that time but may be meaningful in the future. So, the present achievements, no matter how small, may be used as an input for any other work in the future. The analysis of the output must be done on both quantitative and qualitative basis. Some achievements are visible, whereas some are not. Only a practical approach to the analysis of output can give a clear and positive picture of the result of our efforts. This will certainly motivate us for our self-development.

Setbacks

Setbacks are a must in any work and in any venture. We may give it any name, such as problems, hurdles, failures, betrayal, etc., but these are realities of our life. We must admit and accept the uncertainties in each moment and in every sphere of our life. Accidents are not to be considered as surprises, rather to be accepted as a part of the journey of life. Adversities are challenges. Setbacks, or say failures, are the sources of our experience. As the old saying goes, 'Failure is the pillar of success.' Hence, during self-analysis, we must prepare the list of setbacks we have faced in our work. Much emphasis must be given on the nature and cause of our setbacks for its prevention in the future. Negative thoughts should not be generated while assessing our setbacks.

Learning

Life has become so mechanical and commercial that our focus is always on the quantum of achievements. We make all efforts to accomplish the job at hand in time. We get satisfaction when the goal is achieved. But we forget that during the course of action, the work itself teaches us in many ways. Hence, we forget to learn from that work experience. Very few of us realize that we have to learn from each of our actions. It does not matter whether the end result is positive or negative. We get excited when we get the desired results and get depressed in case of setbacks. As a result, we fail to learn from that particular assignment. Learning can only add value to our life. So, during self-analysis, we must make a list of our learnings from each action. Only learning can open a new path for our self-development.

There is no specific time for self-analysis; this can be done before starting a project or after completing it or at the end of the day, before going to bed. This should be a spontaneous process. Self-analysis must be done with a positive attitude and creative thinking. Each one of us can try this and enjoy the result of self-development.

Positive Attitude and Self-motivation

Human being is considered to be the best among all creations. They can decide what is right or wrong and what should be done and when. Because of this thinking power or rationality, human beings have proved themselves as the best creation of God.

Everyone has some good as well bad qualities. According to the proportion of these two qualities, a person is considered either good or bad in the society. But those people who can recognize their own shortcomings and accordingly try to rectify them become successful in life. Everybody has some God-gifted qualities, which can lead him or her towards success.

If somewhere in life we fail, we become discouraged and sad. Suddenly, we feel hopeless and degraded. This way, not only do we lose our self-confidence but also the zeal to work further. It is a negative attitude. This is very dangerous, as it will lead us nowhere in life. So, in any situation, we have to keep a positive attitude.

Whatever problem comes our way, we should never break down, mentally or emotionally, in life. No problem can be solved this way. We should think positively and try to find out some solution. Positive thinking not only strengthens one's self-confidence but also gives encouragement to work with zeal. So, however worse the situation, we should approach it positively.

We should never forget that it is a positive attitude that has been the base of all success stories. After all, we need to remember that we are the best creation of this world, and we have been blessed with many good qualities.

Using our own knowledge, thinking power and self-confidence, we can achieve any heights and lead a better life.

If one concentrates on the following points, he/she can definitely achieve success in life:

- Stamp your goal indelibly on your mind;
- Always picture yourself as succeeding with God's help;
- When a negative thought enters your mind, replace it immediately with a positive one;
- Mentally minimize difficulties and maximize your strengths;
- Deny the power of difficulty over you. Affirm the power of faith to overcome difficulties;
- Believe in yourself;
- Always be genuinely friendly;
- Keep on learning, growing and improving yourself;
- Build a ladder to your dreams with determination, dedication, discipline and positive attitude;
- Practise the greatest of all positive affirmations every day, 'I can do all things through God, who strengthens me.'[1]

---

1. Norman Vincent Peale, *The Power of Positive Thinking*, Volume 2, 2016.

Be the Master of Your Destiny

An interesting fact is that it is easy to prove a lie but very difficult to prove a truth. Similarly, it takes no time to arrive at a negative conclusion. But it takes more time to arrive at a positive one. All these happen in reality, which affects our life, both personal and professional.

No one is perfect. We know this but neither we admit nor realize it. We always try to be perfect and at the same time, expect others to be so. Perfection is a myth. Hence, striving for perfection leads to frustration and all types of negative thoughts. This spreads like a forest fire and damages our life—mentally, physically, spiritually and emotionally. Life becomes a burden and we, a slave to our destiny. If we want to be the master of our fate, we have to practise the following:

Accepting a Situation

We must attune our mind to accept the realities of life. Any situation arising around us is the reality. We cannot dictate our terms for these situations. Complaining about the situation has no meaning at all. Hence, we must accept it positively and start analyzing the process to find out its root cause. Based on that, we can think creatively to arrive at the solutions and chart out the next course of action. On the contrary, if we do not accept the situation and start complaining, we cannot think calmly for a better future.

Accepting a Person

Each one of us is unique. We all differ from each other, in various ways. That is the uniqueness of God's creation. Hence, we must accept each person as he/she is. The problem starts when we look at people from our perspective, but not as they are. Mostly, we start prescribing about the nature or quality of others, such as, he should be like this, and he should not be like this. We don't hesitate to find fault in others and take pride in giving suggestions for their correction. This creates misunderstanding and tension in our relationships. Hence, while dealing with people, we have to bear in mind that we are not dealing with creatures of logic but of emotion.

Accepting Self

Accepting the truth about Self is a tough task. Self-awareness, self-management and self-development get less priority in our life. Mostly, we take ourselves for granted. We invest more time in trying to understand others but less to understand ourselves. Some people are overconfident and over-smart. They think they are superior to others. They never confess their own mistakes, rather justify them. Some people have inferiority complex and consider themselves unfortunate as compared to others. Mostly, they underestimate themselves. They blame their destiny and also, God. Both these are not beneficial to us. We must accept Self as we are. We should not compare ourselves with others. We must understand our strengths and weaknesses, and plan our action based on that. Accepting the truth about Self will lead to a balanced and meaningful life.

The rigidity of the mind, our ego, mental blocks and negative thoughts create hurdles in accepting a situation, a person and Self. In spite of all such roadblocks, if we can practise the above-mentioned actions and sustain them as a habit, we can surely be a master of our destiny.

Changing Our Habits for an Effective Life

Dreams are the driving force of human lives. Is there anyone who does not have dreams? A child or adult, man or woman, poor or rich, healthy or sick, educated or illiterate, powerful or powerless—whatever the state or status, one must have a dream to live for and look ahead in life. Dreams have always been the basis of development. Hence, dreams are essential to improve and enrich our life.

Simply having dreams is not sufficient; we have to put them in action. Dreams are to be converted to reality; that needs sincere effort and hard work. People do dream all the time, but very few put in the required effort to make them come true. We dream about achieving the goal but do not work hard in that direction. Hence, we do not get what we want. Then comes the frustration, tension, worries, depression, stress and all types of negative feelings in life. At the end, we fail to balance our life and create problems for Self and others in the family and society.

We never hesitate to blame others for our failure; rather, we get pleasure in finding fault with others. But in reality, we are the cause of our own failure. Most of us are not prepared to accept this truth. Hence, there is an imbalance most of the time in our life—be it in the family, society or workplace, even inside our own self. The present scenario in our personal and professional life has changed dramatically, beyond our expectations. The norms, structures, nature and system of our family have changed. The principles, ideologies, attitudes, values and goals of our individual life have also changed.

The more we are moving ahead, more are the gaps in our personal life. The work–life balance is at risk. We do not have mental peace. Tension and stress dominate our daily life. We are victimized each moment; the reasons may be different. Hence, we fail to make our personal life effective, in spite of our professional achievements. How do we make our life effective? How do we get out of these mental calamities? How do we expel tension and stress from our mind? How do we stay positive? The answer is very simple. We have to change some of our habits in our daily life. This is not for an occasion only but needs to be put to regular practise, without fail. Let us change our habits as suggested below to make our life more effective:

- When you change your thinking, you change your beliefs;
- When you change your beliefs, you change your expectations;
- When you change your expectations, you change your attitude;
- When you change your attitude, you change your behaviour;
- When you change your behaviour, you change your performance;
- When you change your performance, you change your life.[1]

1. John Maxwell, 'Changing your beliefs starts with changing your thinking,' 22 February 2004.

Can We Stop...? If Not, Then What?

We want everything to work in our favour. And when things do not go in our favour or do not satisfy our ego, we feel very depressed, frustrated and start blaming others for it. We are not prepared to accept all that happen in our life, even events created by nature. We want to change all that exist or happen around us as per our own need. But we never want to change ourselves. Does it not sound very interesting? Hence, let us ask ourselves a few questions, which can help us gauge the reality.

Can We Stop the Rain, a Cyclone or a Tsunami?

Rain, cyclone and tsunami are natural occurrences. In spite of our continuous and dedicated efforts, we cannot stop them. No, we cannot. We need rain and wind, but sometimes they too can create problem. We cannot stop them, but we can think of protecting ourselves with the help of an umbrella, a raincoat or any other shelter as found suitable. We can think of prevention or protection, but we cannot wish them away completely.

Can We Stop an Earthquake?

An earthquake is the disturbance created by an imbalance in nature. No one welcomes it. The damage caused is beyond imagination. We just cannot stop the earthquake. But we can try to repair the damage caused. We need the courage to start life all over again.

Can We Stop a Flood?

Water is life. We cannot survive without water. But excess of water in the river creates flood, something that we cannot prevent. We cannot stop its way. It will occur as destined and lead to great devastation. But we can think of relief, rehabilitation, protection and shelter.

Can We Stop an Accident?

Accidents happen every day, even each moment; it may be physical, mental or spiritual. Sometimes it happens for our faults and sometimes due to others. Whatever may be the reason, we are the victims. We cannot stop it, though we never want it in our life. We can only be careful and take all precautions for their prevention.

Can We Stop Others from Doing Harm to Us?

At any moment, anything can happen to anyone. We may be good to others, but we cannot always expect that others should be good to us too. It all depends on them and how they behave. Others can either help or harm us. We have no control over that. But we can make sure that we never harm anybody. We will never think of creating problems for others, even if we are in trouble. It may sound impossible, but we have to make it possible.

Can We Stop Anybody from Going on the Wrong Path?

There are always two paths before us—the right and the wrong. The selection of the required path depends on the person's need, greed, values, attitude, etc. No one can predict that. Hence, we cannot stop anyone from going on the wrong path, but we can only guide them properly. However, it depends entirely on them to accept our guidance or not.

Can We Change Others?

Change is the universal truth and it is the only thing that will always remain constant. We always think of changing others, but that is very difficult and, at times, it is almost impossible. We cannot change others as we feel or think it to be. But we can only change ourselves. There is also no guarantee that we can change ourselves. Hence, let us try to change ourselves first before we think of changing others.

All said and done, we must realize about our own limitations. Let us accept that reality and then think of going beyond that. When we cannot stop anything, why should we get worried? Worries will never bring us the solution, rather multiply the problems. We must think positive in order to manage or change ourselves, if we wish to accept and accommodate all events in our life effectively. Creative thinking, coupled with a positive attitude, is the only tool to achieve success. However, the choice is always ours.

Beware of Killer Factors in Relationships

Creating a relationship may be very easy and simple, but sustaining it is very tough, painstaking and challenging. Every one of us wishes to build a healthy relationship. No one wants to break a relation or wishes to damage it at any time or under any circumstance. The common idea is to gain from a relation but not to lose one. But in spite of all our effort, a relationship sometimes gets polluted, damaged and broken. This has become a common occurrence in the present society. No one is an exception to this. Each person has experienced this in his/her life.

A healthy relationship is based on many factors, such as mutual understanding, trust, respect, honouring each other's views, sharing and caring, sacrifice and service, accepting both positive and negative aspects of each other, transparency, forgiving, adjustment with honour—the list is endless. The tragedy is that we all wish to have healthy relations but very rarely do we practise the features which enrich a relation and sustain it forever. Thinking beyond Self is the basic foundation for building a trustworthy relation which will never perish, despite all odds. This has been experienced by many people in their life.

Hence, we must be aware of the factors that kill a healthy relationship and disturb the peace in our life. Break-ups lead to complex situations and the loss of mental well-being. Some have the willpower and positivity to absorb the shock of a broken relationship and move on in life. But most of us get affected and suffer for a long period. In order to sustain a healthy relationship, we should be aware of the following killer factors:

Focusing on Self

We mostly focus on self-interest and ignore the interest of others. This happens by default with most of the people. The focus on 'I' creates all hurdles. Some common statements where the focus in entirely on 'I' are: 'I am right, I know everything.' 'I want this.' 'I must win.' 'I will speak first.' 'I must be given importance.' 'I am better than others.' 'I have not made any mistake.' 'I am not properly understood.' 'I am helpful to all but others are not.'

While focusing on 'I', we forget the importance of 'You' and 'We'. In a relation, focus on 'You' and 'We' will facilitate the creation of a bond that is strong and long lasting. But we become so blind and arrogant that we don't recognize the worth of the other person in a relationship. Hence, we must give up the habit of focusing on Self all the time.

Justifying the Mistake

No one is perfect. Each one of us is a blend of positive and negative traits. Human beings are liable to commit mistake.

That is the part of our action. Hence, one must admit his mistake and try to learn from that, so that he will not repeat it again. Furthermore, he will enrich his skill and knowledge from that learning. But mostly, people hesitate to admit their mistake and give justifications to support their mistake. The time and talent they invest in creating these justifications is a waste. Those do not yield any positive result. Instead, they make the relation more complicated and breaks the relation eventually. Committing a mistake is not a crime but not admitting it is really one. Hence, we must make the habit of admitting our mistakes and learning from them.

Blaming Others

Success and failure are two sides of the same coin. We must accept this reality and own the responsibility, especially in case of failure. But usually, the reverse happens. We gladly own the credit in success but do not hesitate to blame others in case of failure. Blaming others is very easy, but the result is very damaging. This attitude of saving our own face by blaming others kills the relation forever. People become so hostile that they go to any extent to harm each other. Instead of finding faults with others, we must find the same in ourselves. That will enrich our relation and enhance the mutual respect and trust. Let us practise this habit from today itself.

Breaking the Trust

A true relationship is based on trust. We must honour that trust and try to sustain it with all sincerity. This is a commitment to each other that we will not break our relation or will not betray each other.

Trust is based on complete acceptance of each other. No one is perfect. When we accept someone, it indicates that we have accepted both his / her positive as well as negative aspects. Trust is not conditional. It is the sign of complete acceptance. When we declare that we have trust in a person, we must not betray it with our misdeeds. People easily break this trust for their petty self-interest. They are neither sensitive about their negative action nor realize that they have committed a crime of betrayal. Rather, they have many reasons to justify their action; the common excuse being that the situation provoked them to do so. No one can convince them, as they have done it willfully.

Being Overconfident

Confidence is good but not overconfidence. Similarly, smartness is good but not over-smartness. Many people exhibit overconfidence or over-smartness. Their conviction is that this is the best way to prove their worth in the society. They claim to be more intelligent than others and think that they can win over others with this attitude. But people around them are not fools—as they consider them to be. In the present society, each person has his / her own way of assessing others and grading them as per their action. Hence, being overconfident will not help us in maintaining a healthy relationship; rather, it will hurt others' emotions and sentiments. We must consider others at par and act accordingly to gain their confidence in us.

Ignoring Mutual Respect

Cohesiveness in a relation is based on mutual understanding and mutual respect. As we wish to get respect and recognition from others in our relationship, others also expect equal reciprocation from us. This is the truth in relationship building, which we forget most of the time. Respect is not demanded; rather, it is commanded. We must behave in such a manner that the other person will willingly respect us. That respect will come from within. Being self-oriented, very often we disrespect others' views on any matter and always give importance to our own views and feelings only. This happens when we take others for granted. This is common behaviour, but it is a hurdle in maintaining a relationship for long. Our own image will be enhanced when we learn to respect others for their positive actions.

Reacting and Concluding

The most dangerous factor is the attitude of reacting and jumping to conclusions. No one is completely good or bad. We may be right or wrong on any occasion. We may differ in our opinion on many issues and may not have mind match. That does not mean that we cannot have a good relationship. Many people react instantly when their views differ from others, or others do not agree with them. Besides reacting very badly, they come to a negative conclusion abruptly without giving much thought on the consequence of such a reaction. The attitude of reacting reflects the ego of that person—that he is always right. This will never sustain a healthy relationship. No one will tolerate this behaviour. Hence, we must not be in a hurry to arrive at a conclusion.

Having a Negative Attitude

The most harmful factor is our negative attitude. This is like a fatal disease. The person having negative attitude will focus on all negative factors in a relationship; this is just like looking at the half-filled glass as half-empty. The thinking, feeling and action will always be directed towards the negative path. All incidences will be interpreted in negative ways. Hence, the conclusion will be negative too. In a relationship, there will be many ups and downs, but those are to be looked at with a positive attitude. This approach will enable us to solve all problems, as and when they arise in a relationship. The person with a positive attitude has the solution to all problems, but the person with negative attitude has no solutions. The best way to maintain a relationship is with the genuine realization of our own action, which will be possible with a positive attitude.

The list of killer factors in a relationship is endless, but efforts have been made to describe the common ones. This will facilitate our realization of the harmful impact of these factors. Genuine realization can bring about a change in our attitude, so that we can enjoy a healthy and long-lasting relationship based on mutual respect.

Trust and Acceptance in Relationships

A healthy relationship with others around us is very vital for a peaceful existence. Be it personal or professional, the significance of relationships has its own worth. Relative and relation or relationship have different meaning. Relative refers to a person connected by blood or marriage. But relation or relationship is the way in which two or more people are connected; it also means the way in which two or more people regard and behave towards each other. They may not be connected by blood or marriage, but the relation is stronger than that. Being a relative is not the only basis of a good relation. He / she may not be your relative, but you may have an honest, decent and worthy relation with him / her. We have enough experience of this in our life.

One of my friends openly expressed his feeling that he does not trust his own son; rather, he has full trust in his close friend. When he confided in me about this, he was not emotional, rather rational. On many occasions, it has been observed that the so-called 'relatives' have betrayed our trust or created many hurdles in our life. Our own blood relations, such as brother, sister, son, daughter, uncle, aunt, and even sometimes, parents become hostile in their behaviour and disturb a peaceful existence. The focus on materialistic goals and selfish motives are the basis of such damaged/broken relationships.

Studies in human psychology, especially on human behaviour, have revealed that trust and acceptance are the major factors in an honest relation. A relationship cannot exist without these between the persons related; that is the lifeline of a well-bonded relation. Similarity of mindset, attitude, emotion, values, ethics, culture, knowledge and skill sets is not enough to build a close and long-lasting relation. The cement that ties the bond is trust and acceptance.

We have to create a climate of trust and acceptance in any relationship. Trust is based on mutual understanding and respect for each other's feelings and views. There should absolutely be no misunderstanding. Trust has to be complete in every aspect. It has to be cent-per cent trust. Very often, we call it 'blind trust', which means there is no room for doubt, confusion or fear. Trust is the binding force in any long-lasting relationship.

Acceptance and trust are complementary to each other. Where there is acceptance, there is trust, and vice versa. One cannot accept the other person without trust and also one cannot trust the other person without accepting him/her. Acceptance also has to come from within, without any precondition. It has to be genuine, without any selfish motive. Complete acceptance means acceptance of both positive and negative traits. Accepting a person as he / she is can only happen if you have that trust. Creating trust and acceptance is a tough task and sustaining that in a relationship is even tougher. We can achieve this if we can keep our conscience clean and head cool, free of all negative thoughts in our life.

Part – 3

Rediscovering Self

Rediscovery of Self

The term 'rediscovering Self' may be difficult to understand, but let us try to grasp its meaning. The journey of life brings about many changes in our thinking, feeling and also, actions. We are subjected to different external as well as internal forces, which alter our thought process and course of action. Hence, there is a need of rediscovering Self. We will be able to have a fair idea of the reality if we can ask ourselves a few questions.

Have We Rediscovered Ourselves?

We claim that we have understood ourselves well, but it is not true. How many of us have rediscovered ourselves in different stages of our life? A deep look inside us will reveal many aspects of our life that are still a mystery.

Have We Redefined Our Roles?

We play many roles in our life, both personal and professional. Many a time, we become overconfident. Emotions and mindsets mislead us to take wrong decisions. We realize that only after the incident. Hence, we must redefine our roles to suit the situation.

What Is the Vision of Our Life?

Each individual must have a vision in life. In fact, most of us have a vision, but it is not clearly defined or documented. Hence, a person without a vision has a meaningless life. Each of us must think creatively and set our vision accordingly.

What Is the Mission of Our Life?

Life has no meaning without a mission. How many of us have clearly defined the mission of our life? The mission is the guiding factor in order to lead an effective life. It controls our thinking, feelings and actions. At each stage of our life, this mission is to be assessed. Our focus must always be on the mission of our life.

What Are the Core Values of Our Life?

Let us be honest to ourselves. How many of us have clearly understood the meaning of the term 'core value'? Have we ever tried to find out what the core values of our life are? Instead, we compromise on them to achieve unethical gains. It is core values that create our identity as human beings.

What Are Our Work Ethics?

Our core values decide our work ethics. The character and personality of a person are built on that foundation. Work ethics create the identity of a person in the society. How many of us are concerned about our work ethics? These are not to be discussed or to be debated but rather, to be put into action.

What Is the Worth of Our Life?

No one appreciates leading a worthless life, but how many of us have ever tried to assess the worth of our own life? Self-assessment is the best way to find out whether you are an asset or a burden to the society. Why should we allow others to find the worth of our life? We must find this out to feel the essence of life. If not done earlier, let us start from today.

What Values Are We Adding to Our Everyday Life?

Day by day, we are approaching the end of our life. We are growing in experience and maturity with age in each aspect of our life. However, we, sometimes, focus more on the growth of our materialistic assets: money, power, position, etc. But have we ever focused on the value addition to our life? To be honest, very few of us must be thinking on this. But this is a priority. We must focus on the values we are adding to our life on a daily basis.

Have We Ever Talked to Ourselves about All These Factors?

We have enough time to discuss various events and issues happening in this world. But it is a tragedy that we do not have the time to introspect. Let us be honest. How many of us self-audit on a daily basis? How many of us talk to ourselves to find our own mistakes? Many of us do not feel the need to talk to ourselves, even if guided to do so. Talking to Self will solve most of our problems.

If Yes, What Are the Outcomes? If Not, When Will We Do That?

A few of us may say that they are talking to themselves or do self-analysis. If this is true, then what is the outcome? Have they changed their own life and motivated others for value addition in theirs? Talking to Self should not be mechanical or to satisfy others. The outcome of this self-audit must be visible. If we have not thought over these matters, the question is: When will we do that? When will we feel the need to rediscover Self?

The Choice is Ours

All said and done, at the end of the day, it is all about enriching our own life, adding value to make it meaningful. These questions are food for thought. The deeper we think on this, the better will be our understanding of Self. Hence, to accept or reject, to realize or forget, to be serious or casual about rediscovering Self, the choice is always ours.

In Search of Self

I have been searching for my true identity since childhood. The question 'Who Am I?' has been bothering me since many years. This is a short and simple question but very thought provoking. I do not know how others look at it, but I do not intend to answer it casually. It needs deep thinking and critical analysis before we come to a conclusion. Does anyone has the right answer to this soul-searching question?

Am I a Name?

I have so many names. As per the official documents, I may have one name, but from my childhood, I have been called by different names by different people; my horoscope name, my certificate name and my nick name being the best examples. I can also change my name legally, anytime in my life. Hence, I am not just a name.

Am I a Designation?

People introduce themselves or get introduced by their designation. Somehow, I feel embarrassed when people introduce me by my designation. They focus on my job description instead of my name. It seems that the designation is more important than the person. So, the person loses all importance when he loses that designation. I no longer work in an organization as an employee. Hence, I do not have any specific designation, still people introduce me as a consultant, specialist, expert, advisor, life coach, mentor, among others. But I feel I am not just a designation.

Am I a Number?

Presently, each one of us is identified by a number; the most common being our mobile number. People take greater care to save the mobile number of a person correctly than his name itself. We are recognized by various types of numbers. If you are in a job, you have an employee number. Other such numbers include ATM card number, PAN card number, bank account number, credit card number, house number, seniority number and many more. It is very interesting to observe that people address others by their surname, instead of their first name. Is it not embarrassing that we call people by their surname but have no interest in knowing their real name? Sometimes, we even misspell or mispronounce the name of others. Presently, people are recognized by a number than their real name. I don't want to be remembered just as a number.

Am I a Machine?

In the present world, we are all struggling for our existence. The competition is so fierce that we have become machines—money-making machines. Professional life dominates our personal life. We are so lost in our professional responsibilities that we have very less time for our personal/family life. We are neglecting ourselves, our family members, relatives, friends and above all, the society that we live in. People have become materialistic and they focus on acquiring power, position, property and money, at any cost. We even want to have everything, at the expense of others' happiness. This is because we have become machines, rather robots. But I will never prefer to be a machine.

Am I a Human Being?

If you ask anyone to define Self, the simple answer will be: 'I am a human being.' But are we all human beings in the true sense? No doubt, we all physically look like human beings, but in action, most of us behave like animals, and even sometimes, even worse. Hence, we cannot claim to be human beings unless we prove that through our actions. Our action is our identity. As we do, so we create our own image. Hence, physically, mentally, spiritually and emotionally, we have to realize this and reflect on our actions. By birth, we may be human beings, but in action, we prove ourselves inhuman. We need to rectify that.

Realizing and Redefining Self

Rediscovering Self is different from understanding Self. Similarly, understanding Self is also different from realizing Self. The reason is very simple. Rediscovering, understanding and realizing are not the same. We study many subjects but understand very few. But understanding can't lead to realization if we do not study the subject deeply. Realization on any subject empowers us to rediscover the truth in our life. Above all, self-realization is the best path towards self-development. Hence, we must make all effort to rediscover Self through self-realization as analyzed below.

Who Am I?

The question seems to be very simple, but the answer is no doubt very difficult and also critical. Let us guess the suitable answer. Is it the name of a person? Is it the designation or the qualification or the family background or the power and position of someone? When one asks this question to Self, the person gets confused about the right answer. The moment confusion sets in and one starts searching for the correct one, we can say the realization has started. It is a challenge to find out our own identity. Everyone should have an exclusive and unique identity. Let us see how we introduce ourselves in an innovative way to the society.

What Is My Role?

This world is a stage and we are merely actors playing different roles. Like a play or movie, our life, too, has a beginning and an end, with a climax or an anti-climax. We play different roles at different places and on different occasions, as per the need of the situation. In the family, a man plays the role of a son, grandson, brother, father, grandfather, uncle, brother-in-law, son-in-law, and so on. And a woman plays the role of a daughter, granddaughter, sister, mother, grandmother, aunt, sister-in-law, daughter-in-law, etc. Similarly, at the workplace, we play the role of a worker, an owner, a subordinate, the boss, a colleague, a union member, a team leader, etc. In the society also, we play different roles, such as that of a friend, guide, well-wisher, godfather, advisor, motivator, trainer, critic, etc.

Each role has its own responsibilities and limitations. Playing the role may seem to be an easy task but playing it effectively, as per the need, is tough and critical; the reason for this being our ignorance about the responsibilities of each role. Our concept on the role we play is not clear; rather, sometimes we become overconfident in playing them. As a result, we do not get the desired outcome, which leads to worries and tension. If we can deeply analyze our role play, we can easily realize the weaknesses in our performance. Hence, we must make our concept clear before playing the roles in our life.

What Is My Goal?

Having a goal is a must in our life, as it acts as the driving force. We all know about the importance of having a goal in our life, but very few are serious in fixing this. Goal setting is an art and must be done very scientifically. Lack of seriousness in setting a goal leads to wrong directions. We may have different goals at different stages of our life. A person may be talented, positive and hard-working, but he/she cannot succeed in life if his/her goal is not fixed. One cannot afford to be superfluous in this aspect. Hence, it is necessary to always ask ourselves on each occasion—'What is my goal?'

What Am I Doing?

This question may seem very practical. Most of us claim that we are aware of our role and goal, but in action we prove just the opposite. This means, our activities are directed in different directions. Our thinking is in one direction but we work towards another. But yet we are overconfident. The contradiction between the goal we have set for ourselves and our actions results in failure, which creates frustration, demotivation, depression and tension. Confidence is good but not overconfidence and smartness is good but not over-smartness. Our word and work must match. Our actions must be directed towards that goal. Hence, it is very practical to ask ourselves—'What am I doing?'

What Do Others Expect From Me?

Human beings are self-centered, by default. By nature, we all expect a lot from others. Our mind is tuned to get the maximum from others. We feel comfortable with them who help us but become hostile to them who do not. The nature of our relation depends on the quantum of our expectations fulfilled by others. In other words, the relation becomes too selfish. That is why there is conflict in most of the families and relations. This can be solved if we give some thought on the expectations others have from us. Once we focus on that and act towards it, the relation will be cordial, peaceful and fulfilling. Hence, while expecting from others, we must also be concerned about others' expectations from us.

Am I Accountable for My Work?

'Accountability' is a word which is rarely honoured in our life. We all claim to be responsible people, but when the question of accountability comes, most of us prefer to be escapists. While taking credit for our work, we step forward; but in case of failure, we run backwards. Responsibility and accountability are two sides of a coin. All of us must be accountable for our work. Whether it is success or failure, we must be accountable for it. We must admit and accept the setbacks or negligence of our responsibility. Generally, people shift the responsibility to others when the issue of accountability arises. This is an act of cowardice and irresponsibility. Hence, we must be bold enough to be accountable for our work. Why not ask ourself: 'Am I being accountable for my work?'

Whom Am I Reporting To?

'Reporting' is a very sensitive and critical term, whether in the family or at the workplace. The general concept is that juniors have to report to the seniors for all their actions and decisions taken. Hence, there is a boss and subordinate relationship. It is also said that the boss is always right. This concept of reporting creates all type of conflicts, confusions and communication gaps, leading to very unhealthy situations and tensions. Instead of the desired benefits, this traditional 'reporting' damages the purpose of our life. But the true reporting is reporting to Self. We must all report to ourselves, to our conscience. Once we start reporting to ourselves every day, rather on each occasion, there will be real joy in our life. We can be properly guided towards our desired goals with due accountability. Hence, let us start reporting to ourselves in the true sense.

What Next?

We have eyes, but we do not have a vision for the future. We usually tend to ignore or overlook the impact of our actions on others. We all know that every action has an equal and opposite reaction. But in practical field, the knowledge of this fact is deleted from our mind. As a result, we involve ourselves in many activities which end in negative results. We realize the truth only after the damage has been done. Hence, it is always wise to ask ourselves 'What next?' before undertaking any work or venture. Prevention is better than cure.

Taking Possession of Self

All over the world, people are possessive about things, living as well as non-living. 'Possessive' has its own definition, but people redefine it in their own way for their own interest. Being possessive may not be harmful per se, but in most of the cases, it has proved otherwise. Being possessive can be interpreted in both positive and negative ways. It entirely depends on the thought, feeling and action of the person.

Being possessive at the cost of others is a crime, but rarely do we realize it. There is no harm in being possessive, but it has to be within limits. When we become possessive for our own interest, we never realize the negative impact of this on others. In such cases, we are enjoying at the cost of others. By the time we realize this, the situation gets beyond our control.

Being Possessive About People

Being possessive is common in all relations, both personal and professional. Parents become possessive about their children, husband about wife, and vice versa. This is also reflected in different relations. When we love somebody, we become possessive about that person. We take the relationship for granted. We try to justify our love for that person. We want him / her to be a person of our choice. We expect the person to do what we think and feel is right. We take them for granted.

In other words, we claim ourselves to be a God for the person. In the process, we ignore the other person's identity, likes, dislikes and also, freedom. We forget to honour the person as a unique creation of God with his / her own thinking, feeling and action. We become so blindly possessive that we even forget the human values. The misunderstanding starts from there, leading to break-up in the relations. It is a common thing, but we hardly make efforts to rectify it.

We are sharp in criticizing others when they become possessive, but when it comes to us, we are prompt in justifying our point. Being overly possessive kills our human values, makes us blind and closes all doors of positive thinking.

Possession of Power, Position and Property

We love power, position and property, so much that we want to achieve them at any cost. This mindset has damaged individual life, family, society and even, the country. The thirst for possession of power, position and property has killed many relationships and sometimes, even taken lives. This is increasing day by day, all over the world. Our life is also affected, directly or indirectly, by this craving for power, position and assets. Everyone realizes this, but when the opportunity comes, one tends to give in to temptation. We only focus on our self-interest and try to achieve the desired goal, at any cost. We simply become blind to the existence of others and their sentiments.

Possession of Self

A very interesting fact is that we never try to be possessive about Self. How many of us have taken possession of Self? How many of us have taken the possession of our thoughts, feelings and actions? We do not have control over our thoughts, feelings and actions, but we want to control others'. By birth, all of us possess many talents. But how many of us have taken possession of those assets? How many of us have utilized those talents in positive ways? On many occasions, we lose control of what we say and our emotions, we feel helpless and also restless.

Sometimes, we openly admit that we have lost control over ourselves. Is it not strange to say that we do not have possession of Self?

We are possessive about people, power, position and property, but unfortunately, we fail to be possessive about Self. We want to change others as per our own perception, but we cannot change ourselves; this is simply because we have not taken the possession of Self. Stress, tension, depression and sorrow are created due to this lack of possession of Self. Let us divert our attention from others to Self. If we can take the possession of Self, we can solve many problems in our life. This does not need any external support; rather, we need our own internal support.

Accepting Self and Others

Acceptance is tough; be it accepting a person, an event, a situation, a concept, a religion or anything else in its true sense. There is an age-old proverb: 'If you accept, it is God, if you do not accept, it is stone.' We can understand the true meaning of 'acceptance' from this saying. It is very easy to say 'I accept', but to show it in action becomes tough. In most of the cases, the word 'acceptance' is used very casually, but its application is a major challenge.

Accepting Others

We all know that we have to accept others, both in our personal and professional life. We cannot live happily and peacefully without accepting others. We have to live with others. We have to work as a team. We have to trust others. We must delegate responsibilities to others. This is the truth. But in most of the cases, we do not accept others as they are. The problem lies in our attitude. We expect that others should be or act as per our suitability. We expect them to be flexible to adjust to our expectations.

Generally, we say, 'Had he been like this, I would have been happy'; but who am I to say this? No one is perfect here. We all have positive and negative qualities. The truth is that each one of us is a combination of both plus and minus factors. Hence, we must accept others as they are—with both sides of the character, good and bad. When I am not perfect, why should I expect others to be so? We all know this, but we do not realize it in its true sense. Instead, we start complaining against others, even God. There is no end to it.

Accepting Self

When we focus on others, we forget ourselves. While discussing the issue of accepting others, most of us forget about self-acceptance. The tragedy is that we have never focused on self-acceptance. To be honest, how many of us have accepted ourselves in the true sense? Self-acceptance is not easy; our ego comes in its way. Besides our strengths or positive qualities, we must accept our weaknesses or shortcomings too. We must have the courage to openly accept our mistakes. But how many of us actually do that?

Instead of accepting our mistake, we give many excuses, defend ourselves by blaming others, even God. We make all efforts to protect ourselves at any cost, even at the cost of others. We become blind to our own mistakes. But why cannot we accept our negative sides? When we take pride in finding mistakes of others, then why not apply the same to ourselves? Understanding the concept of self-acceptance is a challenge. If we want to enrich our life and be at peace, we must focus on self-acceptance.

Acceptance by Others

We all love to be accepted by others at all times, and above all, at all costs. Is it not a very interesting desire? When we are not prepared to accept others as they are under any circumstance, how do we expect that others will gladly accept us at any cost? It is very contradictory. Let us think of our own family. We are not even ready to unconditionally accept other members of the family. There is always a clash of interest between father and mother, brother and sister, father and son, mother and daughter. And the list goes on and on. Acceptance with true love and affection is a myth in our families. Difference of opinion creates such a gap that the family breaks into pieces. All of us will be able to give many such examples.

If we want that others should gladly accept us, then we must first accept others as they are, without any pre-condition. There should not be any ifs and buts in that acceptance. It should be very transparent. No hidden agenda in that, no hypocrisy. These acceptances are complementary to each other. If we accept ourselves and others equally and genuinely, then automatically others will accept us too. Self-acceptance is the first step in accepting others and being accepted by others. If this is achieved, life becomes divine and joyful.

Do We Love Ourselves?

'Do we love ourselves?' I have asked this particular question to the participants in most of my training sessions. The spontaneous answer is always—'YES'. However, the credibility of the answer is to be assessed. I sincerely request the participants to be honest in giving the answer. They seem to be confused with my approach to this question. They remain silent at first, and then, assert, 'Yes, we love ourselves.'

The participants are always very confident in their answer. Then, I ask another question: 'If you love yourself, tell me why? Please give me at least three reasons for it.' The participants start giving the usual responses: 'Who does not love himself or herself?' 'Loving Self is very common,' 'We love Self as we are human beings,' 'We want to live so we love ourselves,' and so on. But I beg to differ with their answers.

The answers are not focused, nor directly related to the question. What I mean to say is that there should be specific reasons why one loves himself/herself. There is no conviction in the answer that they provide. Then, they start realizing that something has gone wrong in understanding the question. When we love someone, there must be some reason for it. Similarly, when we love ourselves, there must be valid reasons for it. It is not that easy to give a genuine answer.

Loving Self seems to be very commonplace and simple but difficult to realize and justify. We are rather overconfident in answering that we love ourselves. We claim that we are taking care of ourselves with full involvement. But my conviction is that we do not genuinely love ourselves. We do not take care of ourselves in the true sense. The truth is that we have never thought much on this issue. We have not talked to ourselves about this, rather, we have taken ourselves for granted.

Let us ask ourselves a question. If we love ourselves, are we making the best investment of our resources, such as our time, talent and energy? Do we also make the best use of other resources available around us? Human life is full of God-gifted resources. We are the master of these resources. But do we make the best investment of these? Honestly speaking, most of the time, we are not able to make the best investment of our resources. Instead, we damage ourselves by wasting our time, talent and energy in all possible ways.

Time is equal for all of us; it cannot be more or less for anyone, under any circumstance. It has no link with power, position, money, religion, education, etc. As we invest our time, so we get the result. It depends on us as to how we invest or waste time. Similarly, the best use of our talents will decide the best output in all our actions. Talents may be used in either positive or negative ways. The best use of our talent in a positive way will give a positive result, leading to success.

The truth is that even we do not have enough knowledge about our own talents. There are so many talents which are not at all used, a few are even misused. Hence, the best use of our talents will make our life meaningful. Then comes our energy. Be it physical, mental or spiritual, energy is vital to our life. The best use of energy will produce the required result in our work. But how many of us are making the best use of our energy in a positive way? If we truly love ourselves, we must make the best investment of our time, talent and energy, at all times, for an effective life. If we are not doing that, it proves that we do not love ourselves. If we love ourselves, we will not waste our lives. It is as simple as that. Now, the choice is ours to decide whether we love ourselves or not.

Knowing It Versus Realizing It

Human being is a finished product, manufactured by God. We consider it as the best creation in this universe, the best ever created by the Supreme Power. The surprising fact is that this finished product does not come with a user manual, as is available for any other finished product. When we debate on this issue in the intellectual forum, all share the view that that the user manual is to be created by the individual. God has provided all resources to an individual to prepare his/her own manual to bring out the best performance.

Now comes a critical question, one which is very difficult to answer. Each individual prepares his/her own manual. But is that enough to lead a person in the right path in life? Can that manual guide the person in a value-based manner for a peaceful and effective life? The manual differs from person to person as regards power, position, caste, religion, financial status, gender, qualification, language, etc. We all belong to one category of God's creation—human being. If so, why are there clearly visible differences in our thought, feeling and action?

Truth has one colour. No one can deny this; but why do we paint different colours to the truth for our self-interest? Why do we twist the situation or interpret words in different ways on different occasions leading to devastation? Why do we plan to harm others, even the creations of God? Why do we love to be negative in our thinking, feelings and actions? Why do we get pleasure in sadistic activities? Can we consider this as the true manual which rarely reflects the activities based on human values? Then how to define human values?

'We all know this,' is a simple statement given by most of us when we discuss human values. Each of us claims with confidence, rather overconfidence, that we know everything. We do not need anyone to teach or preach us on this. It is a wonderful feeling—the feeling that you know everything. Is it true that we know everything? But simply knowing is not enough. It does not add value to our life. Do we really realize that there is a great difference between knowing it and realizing it? And that difference leads to the differences in the thought process and action of human beings.

Hence, knowing it is not enough, we must realize it. Then comes the question: 'How to realize it in true sense?' The answer is very simple. We must put the value-based activities to action. We must convert the ideas to realities, the theory to practical. Not words but actions are necessary. When we convert our thinking into action, we get the result. That is known as our performance. Our performances, or say the achievements, create our identity. We have to evaluate our performance to realize the truth about us. Self-analysis or self-audit is the tool to make us realize the truth and feel the realities in our life. Our concept becomes clear from all angles. Our vision is redefined. The road ahead of us stands distinct—no more confusion, no fear psychosis, no ifs and buts. It is only through realization that we can bring about a change in our attitude, thus leading to changes in our character. The transformation starts in Self after this realization. Let us now start realizing it, instead of becoming complacent in knowing it only.

Focus on Positive Achievements

Our life is neither a business contract nor a commercial transaction. This is the truth. But most of us do not realize the meaning in its true sense. This is clearly reflected in our materialistic attitude. We love to calculate the profit and loss status after each event of our life. We simply treat it as the profit and loss account, and focus on the calculations.

We always focus on the profit. We want the output to be more than the input. Most of the times, we forget how much we have invested and accordingly how much the output should be. When the output is a profit or a success story, we feel fortunate and celebrate. But when the output is a loss or failure, we break down and consider ourselves to be unfortunate. Instead of finding our own fault, we start blaming everybody in this world, we do not spare God too.

Accepting the Reality

We are all intelligent but many a time, we forget the truth of life. We have control over our work, but not the output. The end result in each case is the truth, the reality which we must gladly accept with a positive attitude. We have absolutely no control over the output, or say, the end result. In case the end result is not as per our expectation, we have to accept it positively and start finding the lapses in our input. Instead of finding fault with others for the negative output, let us first find our faults. This will enable us to correct ourselves and find ways to enhance our productivity and performance.

Eliminating Negative Vibes

We may not always get the desired result, even if we work with full involvement and commitment. But the result we get is ultimately the truth at that time, which is to be accepted and analyzed positively for further improvement. The result, be it a profit or loss, never has any negative impact on us. Rather, our attitude towards the result creates negative vibes, which leads to frustration, demotivation, irritation and tension. Polluted mind creates polluted thoughts, which lead to polluted feelings. At the end, this leads to wrong actions. The rigidity in our mind prevents us from accepting the reality in life. We cannot dictate the results. We can only plan and act based on what we think is the best. We must prevent the creation of negativity within us.

Focusing on Positive Achievements

If at all we want to calculate each event as a profit and loss, let us first calculate our achievements. No doubt, the list of our achievements will be longer than that of our failures. The tragedy is that we always focus on what we do not have, instead of the best of what we do have. The few failures overshadow our successes. We print them in our mind and develop a complex within us. This reduces our energy level for facing new challenges in our life. Hence, let us leave the habit of focusing on our failures and start emphasizing on our successes to make our life more peaceful and effective.

Self-audit is the best tool for correcting Self. This is not an overnight task. This is to be practised every day with positive attitude and creative thinking. Be assured, visible changes can be observed if we start focusing from today on our positive achievements only.

Delete, Detach and Dream

Ask anyone a simple question: 'What is your ultimate goal in life?' Most of the people will give a common answer—that they want a peaceful and happy life. Many people may have the goal to be rich and powerful or to achieve excellence in their own field, but each one of them will ultimately search for a peaceful life. At the end of the day, we all want to live in peace.

However, in the present world, life is not peaceful. Rather, it is stressful, with many hurdles, crises, problems, oppositions, uncertainties, challenges, and many more ups and downs. We are used to leading a rough life, day after day. We all know that life is simple, but we make it complicated. We are responsible for everything that happens in our life, good or bad.

The interesting fact is that we all want peace, but we rarely adopt the path that leads to it. No doubt, very few people achieve it. But those who are caught in the crossword puzzle of life, sandwiched between need and greed, make their life even more stressful.

Stress and peace are the two sides of the same coin. We have to live with that, but we must find out the ways and means to manage stress and to be at peace in all situations. Over the years, many methods have been prescribed by different schools of thought to make our life peaceful. However, we can try a very simple process of 'Delete, Detach and Dream' to manage stress and to lead a peaceful life.

Delete

In spite of our efforts to lead a peaceful life, there will always be disturbances created by events or people around us. Most of the times, we do not have any control over them. Life is unpredictable. Hence, the best solution is to 'delete' those events or people from our mind. The computer has a Delete key which proves that certain items are to be removed in order to make your work comfortable. Accordingly, we must have the habit of deleting those unwanted elements from our life too.

Detach

With reference to the act of deleting, we must admit that there are certain unwanted elements in life that cannot be deleted at all. They can be considered as necessary evils. We can choose to be detached from those elements, since we cannot delete them. This will be the best practice to protect ourselves from being affected by those negative elements. In spite of our effort to steer clear of those negative factors, most of the time, they prevail on our day-to-day life. Negative factors are always there around us. We can neither delete nor change them; it is better to change ourselves. The best method is to 'detach' ourselves from those. Hence, delete and detach are two strong weapons needed for our mental peace.

Dream

The best medicine for leading a stress-free and peaceful life is to 'dream'. We must exercise our creative ability to dream big. Positive dreams can make us more energetic, vibrant and confident. Keeping our cool amidst all provocations is necessary for leading a peaceful life. Dreams can keep us alive, amidst all negative forces. Dream, dream and dream till you convert those into a reality of your life.

This simple method of delete, detach and dream can solve many problems in our life. Let us practise it from today and see the results.

Celebrating Life

Celebration is a part of our life. We love to celebrate specific events and special occasions—be it a birthday, an anniversary, New Year, or any other new achievement or religious function. There is no end to the list of events that call for celebration. We invest our time, money and energy in those celebrations. The purpose of celebration is to enjoy and be happy. In many cases, the celebrations become ceremonial; the enjoyment or happiness does not sustain for a long period.

But the fact is that most of the time, we celebrate for the sake of it; we do that to satisfy someone else but not ourselves. The enjoyment, happiness, relaxation and mental satisfaction are lost in the process of celebration. Then why should we have such celebrations which do not add value to our life? The reality is that we cannot avoid such celebrations. Can we, therefore, think of creative ways to add value to celebrations? Enriching Self to lead a quality life should be the purpose of all activities.

Let us celebrate our life each day, each hour, each minute and above all, each event. Be it success or failure, we must celebrate with equal importance. Accepting the realities in our life with a smile is the best way of celebrating life. Embracing uncertainty and accepting change lead to celebration of life. Life is to be accepted as it is, with a positive attitude. We celebrate all new achievements in our life. So why not search for the newness even in our daily life? We can find the following reasons to celebrate each day.

Birth

Every day, we have the arrival of a new life, reflecting the beginning of a new life. Each day brings in its wake many new activities and adventures. We have to feel this newness and accept it with a smile. The feeling of a new arrival and new life each day will enable us to celebrate life.

New Goals

We must set new goals for ourselves. That will give us new directions, new dreams, new hopes and new horizons. New goals will always motivate us to celebrate life and move ahead with renewed zeal.

New Challenges

Each day, we will have new challenges with new goals to be achieved. Challenges are part of our life. Challenges are to be met with courage and confidence. Winning over the challenges, even minor ones, will create the climate for celebrating life.

New Actions

Creative thinking will enable us to find new strategies to face challenges and achieve goals. Actions need to be innovative, moving in new directions. Better ways of doing things will yield better results. Our actions will create our identity and reflect our personality. We can celebrate life with new actions.

New Experiences

Experiences will be gained through our actions. New actions lead to new experiences. The more we work, the more experiences we have. New experiences empower us for a new life, to face new challenges, to set new goals. New experiences add value to our life, giving us reasons to celebrate.

New Learnings

We learn from our experience, which leads to visible changes in our behaviour and capability. New actions lead to new experiences, which result in new learning. Learnings are lifetime assets that make our foundation strong. Learning enriches our life.

New Developments

Learning leads to our all-round development. Development is the symbol of growth, the ultimate outcome of our sincere efforts to improve the quality of our life.

New Value Addition

Value addition to our life is the ultimate goal. Life without values has no meaning. Each day creates the opportunity for value addition. We must have the skill to identify and make the best use of it. Self-renewal leads to value addition. Altogether, it is a new celebration.

Each day in our life is filled with opportunities for new celebrations. Creating newness in all events and all moments is the charm of life; that makes our life happy, joyful, meaningful, peaceful, eventful and valuable. The ultimate goal is to keep smiling and sustain the positivity every day. If we accept it as a truth, let us celebrate life every day.

Part – 4

Empowering Self

Empower Yourself First

All said and done, empowerment is possible if the need for it emerges from that person himself. In other words, if we feel the need and have the will to be empowered, we can work in that direction. In most of the cases, the need may be there, but there is the lack of will. We are not even in a position to recognize our own talents and our inner strengths, which can otherwise lead us to greater heights, if utilized effectively. In order to achieve this, some of the basic human skills are to be developed first. These skills will act as the foundation for the empowerment of Self in any field. Details of these basic human skills are described below, which should be inculcated in our mind and practised on a priority basis.

Thinking

Thinking is the most important activity in our day-to-day life. Any job done without thinking either ends in disaster or yields no result. The common saying is that 'think before you leap'. Hence, we have to inculcate the habit of thinking before taking any decision in our life. Think, think and think. This will help us find out the solution to any problem. In our thought process, what matters most is our attitude. Hence, we have to think with a positive attitude. It is only we, and no one else, who can put us in a positive mood.

Asking

No one is expected to know everything on all subjects. In order to get correct information, we have to ask others who have the expertise in the field or we have to look for the right information using other sources. This will not only enrich our knowledge but also enable us to increase our thinking process for taking the right decision on any issue. So, we should never hesitate or feel shy to ask others, as per our need. If we stop asking, then we stop learning and also stop growing. Hence, let us not hesitate to ask questions, when in doubt.

Doing

We can achieve success if we do the work. Dreams can only be fruitful if converted to action or reality. If we do the work, we get happiness (in case of success) or we get the experience (in case of failure). This experience strengthens our confidence to do the work in a better way for a better result. Hence, we must act once we have made up our mind. Focusing on ifs and buts will never help us succeed in our life. Hence, let us start acting on our goals before the ideas perish.

Communicating

Communication is the backbone of all activities in our life. Effective communication leads the way to the solution of any problem. So, one should effectively communicate the inner feelings, thoughts and emotions. This will make the process of reaching the goal much easier. If we do not communicate about our needs at the right moment, in the right place, then we do not get it. No one can help solve our problem if we do not express it openly. Keeping quiet will not solve the problem. Hence, we must know how to communicate, when to communicate and whom to communicate with. We should not be aggressive nor submissive but assertive in our communication.

Facing the Problem

Our life is never a bed of roses. There will always be problems or hurdles in any work we do, which we can neither avoid nor neglect. We have to take it as a part of the work process, of the work experience. So, instead of considering the problem as a 'problem', we have to accept it as a challenge, and make all efforts to face it head-on. Once we have the courage to face the challenge, we can find out the ways and means to overcome it too. As a result, we achieve success and also increase our self-confidence to face more challenges; this again depends on our willpower. Hence, let us learn to face the challenges and solve the crises that life throws at us.

Hope and Hunger: The Tools for an Effective Life

Life is precious for all. Each one of us wishes to lead a meaningful, joyful, eventful, resourceful and powerful life. Each human being wishes to lead a fruitful life, from all angles. Effectiveness of life also has different meanings for people with different mission, vision, values and ethics. But, when we focus on the positive aspect of effectiveness in life, we think of a life which is fruitful, peaceful and joyful.

But how to make life effective, in spite of so many hurdles? Each person has his own way of achieving the desired goal to make life fruitful. But the truth is that all that glitters is not gold. Here, we will discuss the two major factors i.e. hope and hunger, which can help make our life effective.

Hope is the lighthouse in our life. It facilitates our living amidst all odds and oppositions. But in most cases, we lose hope and lead a stressful life. We find darkness all around us and fight hard to survive. Hence, we have to create hope in all situations and at all times. This can only be possible if we practise the following actions in our life without any compromise:

- ✧ Sustaining a Positive Attitude;
- ✧ Building Trust in Self and the Supreme Power;
- ✧ Dreaming with a Vision.

Our attitude may be positive or negative, depending on the event or situation. But we have to convert the negative attitude to a positive one, at any cost. Negative attitude must not be encouraged under any circumstance. Positive attitude will enable us to create hope in our life for a bright future. A positive attitude can keep hope alive. Hence, we must sustain our positive outlook.

Trust in Self and in the Supreme Power is the foundation for creating hope in life. The force within us must say 'Yes I Can Do It'. The 'can do' attitude reflects our trust in Self and in the Supreme Power. We must build this trust and make all efforts to keep it alive. Trust creates a Divine force within us and empowers us to create hope, amidst all failures. Hence, we must sustain our trust in ourselves and in the Divine force at all times.

There cannot be any hope without a dream. One must have a dream, coupled with a vision in life. This dream can be brought to reality based on the foundation of hope. Where there is a dream, there must be a hope to achieve it. A dream and hope are two sides of the coin. Each person must have a vision in life, which will act as the driving force.

All said and done, hunger is the basic ingredient for making life effective, meaningful, joyful and fruitful. A person without hunger will never go out in search of food. Here, the word 'hunger' is not the hunger for food but the hunger to make the life effective. It indicates the acute need for making life meaningful. Food for thought is the basic need for visualizing a bright future in life. We must create that hunger within us and empower us with the hope to achieve that vision, in spite of all hurdles. Hunger will drive us ahead and hope will facilitate the achieving of the end result. Hunger without hope has no meaning and hope without hunger has no result. Hence, we must create hunger in the mind and hope in the heart to make our life effective from all angles. Those who have experienced it in their life are the role models for us to change our life accordingly.

Learning the Art of Learning

We all have dreams in our life. We also consider them as our goals, short term or long term. We make all efforts to achieve our goals or change our dreams to reality, as early as possible. But many a time, it does not happen as per our expectation. This creates frustration or negative vibration in our mind. Then, we start blaming others, sometimes even God. But let us ask ourselves: 'Why do such situations arise?' The answer is very simple. Our efforts perhaps lack something: proper planning, sincere execution, commitment, dedication, a professional approach, adequate investment of time, talent and resources, or self-analysis.

Learning is an Art

It has been observed in many a social research that there is no enrichment of effort we put in any action due to the lack of proper learning on the subject or in the area of activities. There is a basic need for improvement in our efforts to achieve our dreams/goals. This is only possible through continuous learning. Learning is easier said than done. We may say that learning is an art. Each one of us knows very well that without learning we cannot climb the ladder of success or growth. But very few of us realize it.

Hunger for Learning

As we have mentioned above, learning is an art. Hence, we have to learn the art of learning. This can only be possible if we sincerely feel the need for learning. We may say it in a different way—that we must have the hunger for learning. If one does not have the urge to learn, then learning will not be effective. Learning for learning's sake or for getting a certificate/degree will not be of any use in enhancing our performance. We need not learn to impress anyone or to create a false image of a learned person; neither of these cases will benefit us. Hence, we must learn the art of learning sincerely, so that we get the maximum advantage from it in enriching our life—both personal and professional.

Learning from Our Mistakes or Failures

We hope for success in all our endeavours and celebrate when it happens. But in case of failure, we get depressed and draw all negative conclusions. Generally, we do not learn from our failures, which is the greatest opportunity to learn and enrich our skill and knowledge. Those are fortunate who learn from their mistakes and failures, and invest that learning in their future efforts. This is what shapes their actions and achievements. Learning from one's failure depends on the attitude of that person. One has to develop and maintain that positive attitude of learning from own mistakes and of empowering Self for further improvement. Hence, failure is neither a defeat nor a setback, rather an opportunity to learn and mature.

Learning from All

There is no limit to learning. We can learn from all events, all people and at all times in our life. There is no boundary for learning. There is no fixed agenda in learning. Irrespective of gender, age, caste, religion, language, country, education, richness, poverty, power and position, we can learn. But there is a condition; we must learn the positive qualities instead of the negative ones. We are always amidst people and have the opportunity to interact with different types of people on varied areas of activities. Hence, we have ample chances for learning from others, provided we have that hunger for learning. Each human being has positive talents, traits and many experiences. They can be the source of learning for others. Hence, we should not have any mental block regarding the source of learning. Learning can happen anywhere and from anyone. Once we learn from others, we become the source of learning for others, and this continues forever.

Learning is the only way to enrich our knowledge base and skill set. This will enable us to enhance our performance and lead a fruitful and meaningful life. In order to make it happen, we have to learn the art of learning. There is neither any alternative nor any shortcut to our self-development. Hence, let us start learning the art of learning from today itself, without any compromise.

Embracing the Reality with a Smile

The reality is the very truth of life. Despite realizing it, we are not mentally prepared to accept it. What we imagine is a dream, but what takes place is the reality. Hence, the reality matters, not the dream.

However, dream is also a must in life. One cannot live without a dream. Our creative thinking leads to dreams, which shape our goals in life. Dreams drive us on the path of development, but many a time, most of us love to remain in the world of dreams and fantasy. Being confined to dreams only creates frustration, tension and demotivation.

It is only when our dreams are converted to reality through active work that they take on a meaning. Being able to turn dreams to reality is a sign of a leader. After all, achievers are performers. Their productivity leads to production. They are role models.

Those who are opportunists or escapists are not prepared to take real risks in life, face any challenge or commit to convert their dreams into reality. They love to live in a dream world, in their comfort zones. They want to achieve the maximum output with minimum input. Hence, success eludes them and neither they admit nor accept their lapses. Instead, they start blaming others—the system, the society, the government and eventually, God. No doubt, these are all out of frustration. People with such negative attitude and an inflated ego can never add value to themselves or to the society.

Sometimes, even if we make all sincere efforts, we do not get the desired results. In spite of our commitment, hard work, devotion and dedication, the output is not as per expectation. Generally, this leads to frustration, depression and tension. The ones with a positive attitude and a balanced mindset take such failures with a smile and accept this as a reality.

But most of the people are not able to accept this reality positively. Instead, they express their frustration by saying things such as: 'I did not expect it,' 'I am unfortunate,' 'It was not expected of him/her,' 'I am having a bad time,' 'My luck did not favour,' and many such negative statements.

The truth is that we cannot dictate the output, we only have control over our inputs. We have control over our actions but not the result. What has happened is the reality and we must embrace it with a smile. If at all we are not content with the result, we may review our action and plan in a better way to get the desired result the next time. There is no limit to improvement. All said and done, what happens at the end is the reality of life. We must develop the habit of embracing the reality, so that we can lead a peaceful and balanced life. The ultimate goal for all of us is to have mental peace. Embracing the reality with a smile will enable us to achieve that ultimate goal in life.

LOVE: A Skill for Effective Communication

Love is the binding force in all aspects of our life. Love in our life is like fuel to a vehicle. Love is a must for Self as well as for others. Love is the truth in our life, starting from birth till death, and even after that. Love is the light in darkness. Love is the path leading to all destinations. Here, we will discuss how love is the means to effective communication. Love in communication stands for Listen, Observe, Visualize and Express.

Listen

The most important factor for effective communication is active listening. Mostly, we do not have the patience for active listening—listening with concentration or empathy. Listening is an art that we have to learn and develop. The general human tendency is that we expect others to listen to us carefully, but we do not do the same to others. This leads to communication gap, both in our personal as well as professional life. Hence, we must put emphasis on active listening. For listening, we need not only ears but also eyes, a mind and a heart.

Observe

In any conversation, we generally listen to verbal words and forget to observe the non-verbal cues. When we speak, we not only communicate through words but also non-verbally through our gestures, our posture and our body language. Generally, in all communications, the non-verbal expressions play a greater role than the verbal ones. Hence, the focus must be on observing the non-verbal cues as well. Many a time, there is a contradiction between the words being uttered and the non-verbal cues. We say 'Yes' in words but the expression on our face indicates otherwise. If we do not observe the non-verbal expression, then we fail to achieve effective communication and also to read between the lines. So, while listening, we must observe the body language of the person as much as what is being said to decipher the accurate meaning and purpose of the conversation.

Visualize

Active listening with minute observation of non-verbal cues will enable us to understand the message of the communicator. Understanding the message clearly is not an easy task. This depends on many factors relating to the communicator and the receiver. Many a time, we go by the words and misinterpret the entire communication. Hence, we have to go by the meaning behind the words. This can only be possible if we can make efforts to visualize the meaning of the message. We fall short of words to clearly communicate the message we have thought of passing on to others. There may be many communication barriers, starting from the attitude of the person, the situation, time, place and many other external factors.

It has been observed that we think of communicating a particular message, but end up communicating just the opposite. The defect may occur either in proper encoding of the message by the communicator or in decoding of the message by the receiver. Hence, we have to make all efforts to visualize the true meaning of the message, considering the prevailing situation and other factors related to that communication.

Express

Listening, observing and visualizing will empower us to express our feelings, thoughts or any message effectively, without any communication gap. Expression depends on our effective understanding of the message received. Many a time, we communicate to impress than to express. The focus must always be on the effective expression of our thoughts, feelings or information. This needs proper thinking, analyzing our feelings and then encoding of the message in the right format and sending it through appropriate medium to the receiver. There are many people who cannot express themselves properly, even in their personal life. For example, many people find it very difficult to say 'no'. Being able to say 'no' with a smile is an assertive way of communication without hurting others. The way of expression matters a lot in effective communication. Even the unpleasant messages can be expressed in very creative ways for easy acceptance by the people involved. Reacting and responding are two different ways of expression. The difference in impact can be easily observed from the feedback of the receiver. Hence, we must be very careful in our way of expression. What we say may not be that crucial but how we say is the most vital factor in effective communication.

Now, we know the importance of LOVE as the correct path to effective communication. Listening, observing, visualizing and expressing are the four pillars of effective communication. We must develop our skill for active listening, minute observation, creative visualization and assertive expression, so that we can make our communication effective.

Practising the five 'L's

Our life is very precious and so we wish to make it meaningful and peaceful. Each one of us has many dreams and plans to enjoy life, till the very end. No one is willing to accept any adversity, discomfort or obstacle in the path of achieving a joyful life. We do not want tears but smiles. We wish to convert our dreams to reality smoothly. We are eager to gladly accept all positive factors in life but not the negative ones. By default, the human mind is tuned to this type of attitude and mindset. This is natural. We have to find the right course of action as per the goal. Hence, we have to realize this basic truth of life and practise the five 'L' factors to make our life meaningful.

Love

Love is a positive force, even among animals. Life is meaningless without true love. Presently, love is based on self-interest, commercial motives, materialistic gains and negative attitude. Hence, the concept of love is skewed for most of us. We must understand and realize the meaning of true love, selfless love and the divinity of love. First, we must love Self and then, others. Love must be the foundation of our life. If we love Self, then truly we will never waste our time, talent and energy. Love and concern for others will solve many problems. Love will enrich our life and make it meaningful.

Leave

Emotional attachment with all living and non-living objects never allows us to be detached from them. We are overtaken by our need and get lost in our greed. We become possessive and try to hold onto everything that we feel we need. But the truth is we have to leave behind many things if we truly wish to move ahead on the path of progress. We often nurture many negative thoughts, which damage our overall attitude and behaviour. We have to forgive others' mistakes and leave behind our anger, grudges and jealousy, so that we can lead our life peacefully. If we love Self, we have to leave many things behind and enrich our life with more positive forces.

Look

We have eyes to see but many a time, we fail to see the reality. We become very casual in our observation and jump to conclusions. We must have the foresight to look beyond all physical boundaries. We must have the ability to look beyond the mundane. There is a saying: 'Please do not read, just read between the lines, do not just go by the words, go beyond the meaning of the words.' Our mature and pragmatic observation can guide us properly in the right direction.

Learn

Learning is an art. It is a never-ending process. There is no particular source or place to learn. We can learn from everyone, irrespective of their age, religion, cast, education, power, position or money. We can learn from our success as well as our failure. True learning cannot be achieved under pressure. We must have the need or hunger for learning, which actually comes from within. This will decide how much we can learn and put that learning into action for the benefit of Self and others.

Live

There is a great difference between living a life and merely existing. Many people simply exist for the sake of it. They do not realize the meaning of living a life. We have to prove our worth through our actions. We are born as human beings but act like animals, sometimes inferior to them even. Most of us wish to live a life but act just the reverse. At the end, their life becomes a burden. Hence, if we wish to live a life, we have to invest our time, talent, energy and other resources positively and creatively. Besides, we have to give up our ego, mental blocks, rigidity of mind and all the negative factors which prevent us from living a fruitful life.

The Path from Thought to Action

Our actions shape our destiny. Our words have no meaning without proper action. Our actions also reflect our thoughts and create our identity. All achievements in our life are based on our actions. Hence, we should be always action oriented. Actions may be positive or negative, productive or unproductive. In order to make our action positive, productive and creative, we have to explore the path from thought to action.

Thought

The foundation of any action is the creation of an idea. Our mind has the power and ability to think, even faster than a computer. Our thoughts have no limit. They can be productive or unproductive. When we think casually, it is unproductive. But when you think deeply and seriously, it becomes productive. One may use it positively or negatively. This ability to think, when used positively and creatively, generates greater avenues for better results. Any action taken without careful thinking never yields positive results. Hence, we must keep our head cool and focus on making the best use of our thinking ability for better results. Thought is the first step on the path leading to action.

Realization

Thought leads to realization, which is the critical analysis of any idea or event or any issue. Realization will be effective when thinking is critical, lateral, creative and positive. One has to focus on both positive and negative sides of an issue in the process of analysis. There is great difference between knowing and realizing. We may have knowledge about any subject, but it has no utility if we do not realize the inner truth relating to the application of that knowledge. Hence, knowing is not enough; it has to be combined with realization. Only a mature person can grasp the significance of realization, which purifies the mind and results in learning. Realization by Self is the second step on the path leading to action.

Conviction

Realization leads to conviction. One has to be convinced about the truth behind the action. Many a time, we are misguided by others or biased on any subject or event. Sometimes, owing to external pressure also we accept the views of others without proper analysis and realization. We realize the mistakes at a later stage, when the damage has already been done. Hence, we must be convinced about the reality on any issue with proper realization. One should not take any step forward without being convinced and without proper information. Our inner self must be convinced about the truth, which will, in turn, enrich our confidence and the willpower to take any decision. Convincing Self is the third step on the path leading to action.

Decision

Conviction leads to decision. Once we are convinced, it becomes easier to take the right decision. The inner power empowers us to take the decision positively and with confidence. Many a time, we take decisions based on our emotion or excitement; this is misleading. The right decision at the right time gives the right result. There should be no bias, no hurry, no emotion, no greed and no excitement while taking a decision. Decision has to be positive, productive and thoughtful. Even with all precautions, we may take a wrong decision, but that can be corrected with proper realization and conviction. Taking a positive decision is the fourth step on the path leading to action.

Action

Decision leads to action, which shapes the course of our life. Our action creates our identity in the society and reflects our true self. Our action may enrich or damage our life. Hence, actions should be based on positive and thoughtful decisions. Actions must be positive, productive, creative and beneficial to all. Our actions are considered as our performance that enhances the growth of our life. Actions lead to further action by others around us. As we sow so we reap. Every action has an equal and opposite reaction. Hence, we must be very careful in how we act.

Exploring the path from thought to action is a difficult task but not impossible. Once we make it a habit, we will be empowered to take the right action for positive and productive results. This will make our life meaningful and peaceful. Let us explore it more and more for a better life.

Experimenting with the Realities of Life

It is very true that 'easier said than done'. It is easy to talk on a subject or give advice to others. But it is very tough, rather painful, to accept the harsh realities of life. Evaluating an incident in someone's life, from a distance, is not at all difficult. We do not hesitate to give our views, which may be worse or can cause further damage. But when it comes to our own life, we have many explanations, excuses or justifications, which may not be acceptable to others. We do not care about others' acceptance or views on that, rather we never hesitate to blame others for those negative events that happen in our life.

Honestly speaking, we all know that there is a huge gap between the dreams and the realities of our life. We have many desires, aspirations, expectations and dreams in every aspect of our life. We never stop preparing the list of our goals, even though we know very well that those are not practical at all times. We have experienced that in the past in our own and also others' life. One may then ask the questions: 'Why do we not learn from those events?' 'Why do we not realize the truth and accept the reality?' We know a lot but realize very little. Hence, we suffer for our own miscalculations and misjudgements.

We plan, we dream, we even expect the unexpected and then at the end, we fail to achieve the target that was believed to be within our reach. We suffer setbacks; we suffer physically, mentally and spiritually, even sometimes incurring a loss beyond imagination. Financial setback can be restored but what about the emotional and social damages that ruin the strength of our mind and body? Having experienced such grave situations in our life, we rarely realize the truth and practically change ourselves in order to avoid such happenings in future. We realize it for some limited period of time and then repeat the same mistake, knowingly or unknowingly, with many explanations readily available for others' queries. This is the truth of life.

Now the question is: How long will we be experimenting with the reality in our life? Where is the end to such experiments with reality and at what cost? Can anyone give a value-based appropriate answer to this question? This is a very common but tough question. Each one of us is experimenting with many realities every day in life and forced to accept the results, be it positive or negative. But do we really learn anything valuable from those experiments? If at all we do learn, do we put them in action? There is no end to such questions. In reality, it will be better to ask these questions to ourselves only and make all efforts to find out the pragmatic answers from our inner self. Let us start this experiment with ourselves from today till we find a new chapter in our life. However, the choice is ours.

The Choice is Always Ours

Our life is a result of the choices we make. If we do not like the pattern of life we are leading, then it is time to start thinking of a better choice. Our life is ours. Choices are also ours. We think, feel and decide. The sense of accountability for all actions in our life is also ours. Hence, we should never blame anyone for any failure in our life. We all wish to lead a better life. Each of us dreams of having a better tomorrow. But who will make this happen? Who will take the responsibility of making our future better than the present?

The answers to the above questions are very simple. We have to own the responsibility of building our life as per our own dream. Very rarely do people realize this truth. There are a few basic factors which we all have to realize and accept without any compromise. The truth is, there is no fixed formula or magic trick to build a better life; there are no shortcuts either. We have to think, feel and act to build a better life with the following roadmap.

- Fix a goal (short and long term) and focus on that;
- Prepare a work plan and work on it to reach that goal;
- Review (self-audit) the work process and progress on daily basis;
- Admit and learn from mistakes/failures, without blaming others;
- Refine and redesign the work plan and processes as per learning;
- Take risks, face challenges and embrace uncertainties positively;
- Consult other resourceful persons with an open mind to facilitate learning.

The above factors are most crucial in building a better life. Dreaming of a better future is not a mistake but not preparing ourselves accordingly is. Hence, if our dreams are not fulfilled, we invite all frustration, depression, tension, stress, diseases, evil thoughts, and the list never ends. But the tragedy is that very rarely do people blame Self for these misdeeds. Most of us blame others and even God, for all negative events in our life. Isn't that strange? Now, the question arises, how to realize the truth and act accordingly? The answer is also very simple. We have to get rid of the 'I' factor (i.e. our ego), mental blocks, rigidity of mind and negative thoughts.

Thinking about and realizing these factors are not enough. We have to start acting on it. However, the choice is always ours.